Celebrity and Fame

Judith Anderson

amicus

Published by Amicus
P.O. Box 1329, Mankato, Minnesota 56002

Printed in the United States of America at Corporate Graphics, in North Mankato, Minnesota.

Published by arrangement with the Watts Publishing Group Ltd., London.

Library of Congress Cataloging-in-Publication Data

Anderson, Judith.
  Celebrity and fame / by Judith Anderson.
      p. cm. -- (Media power)
  Summary: "Discusses the media treatment of celebrities and famous people worldwide,
  including issues of media pressure, privacy, discrimination, and scandals"--Provided by publisher.
  Includes index.
  ISBN 978-1-60753-112-8 (library binding)
  1. Celebrities in mass media--Juvenile literature. 2. Mass media and culture--Juvenile literature.
  3. Journalistic ethics--Juvenile literature. I. Title.
  P96.C35A54 2011
  302.23086'21--dc22

                                                          2009051451

Series editor: Julia Bird
Design: Nimbus Design

Picture credits: Stuart Atkins/Rex Features: 19; Jean Paul Aussenard/Getty Images: 33; Matt Baron/BEI/Rex Fea-
tures: front cover; Beretta/Sims/Karins/Rex Features: 20; Bettmann/Corbis: 10, 11; Stewart Cook/Rex Features: 37;
Everett Collection/Rex Features: 12; Lenny Furnman/Getty Images: 34; Getty Images: 26; Fiona Hanson/PA/PAI: 30;
Jim Hutchison/Daily Mail/Rex Features: 16; Ikon Pictures Ltd/Rex Features: 13; KPA/Zuma/Rex Features: 9; Barry
Lewis/Corbis: 8; John G Mabanglo/epa/Corbis: 22; Ken McKay/Rex Features: 27; Ray Mickshaw/American Idol/Getty
Images: 31; Yui Mok/PA/PAI: 32; Most Wanted/Rex Features: 28, 29; Offside/Rex Features: 40. Masatoshi Okauchi
/Rex Features: 17; PA Archive/PAI: 21; Michelly Rail/WirePhoto/Getty Images: 38; Reuters/Corbis: 14, 24; Rex Fea-
tures: 23, 36; Stefan Rousseau/PA/PAI: 35, 41; Sipa Press/Rex Features: 25; Jim Smeal/ BEI/Rex Features: 18; Trinity
Mirror/Mirrorpix/Alamy: 15; Tim Whitby/
Getty Images: 39.

1212
32010

9 8 7 6 5 4 3 2 1

Contents

Media and Celebrity 8

The First Celebrities 10

Changing Attitudes 12

Playing the Fame Game 14

A Match Made in the Media 16

Fifteen Minutes of Fame 18

Press Intrusion 20

A Step Too Far? 22

Privacy Laws 24

Lies, All Lies! 26

A Public Fascination 28

Celebrity and Me 30

Identity Crisis.........................32

Taking Sides..........................34

Child Stars...........................36

Doing Good 38

The Future of Celebrity 40

Glossary 42

Further Information...................43

Index 44

Media and Celebrity

Actors, rock stars, sports stars, beautiful people, and rich people—we read about them in magazines and watch them on TV. They are featured in advertisements, gossip columns, and blogs. Sometimes they seek the media spotlight, and sometimes they are exposed by it. These people are celebrities—stars of the media—and like it or not, they help to drive a vast media industry.

Made for Each Other

The media needs celebrities to help sell newspapers and magazines, attract audiences, and create income from advertising. Celebrities, meanwhile, need publicity. They need to be noticed, written about, photographed, and filmed to maintain a high profile and promote their latest ventures. All of this is made possible by the general public. To learn about celebrities, people buy magazines, watch TV, go to the movies, and buy celebrity-endorsed products.

Actress Sienna Miller poses for the cameras at the Venice Film Festival, promoting her latest film.

A Competitive Industry

The media is a huge, global industry. Magazines, newspapers, TV shows, blogs, and web sites are in competition with each other for a share of the audience. One way to increase that share is to be the first with a celebrity story or to have exclusive images or information that no one else has used.

Perez Hilton writes a celebrity gossip blog with an emphasis on rumor and speculation as well as fact. He posts previously unseen video footage of stars and has been accused of many breaches of privacy and copyright. However, claims that his web site is "Hollywood's most hated" simply increase its popularity.

Case Study: The Paparazzi

Photographers pursue celebrities in the hope of an exclusive picture that they can sell to the media. Those who earn a living in this way are known as paparazzi, or "paps." Australian Darryn Lyons set up his Big Pictures agency in 1992. Often referred to as "Mr. Paparazzi," Lyons is now famous in his own right for selling revealing images of celebrities such as soccer player David Beckham.

Perez Hilton's blog has made him as famous as some of the celebrities he writes about.

The First Celebrities

Famous people have always been written about and admired. Before newspapers, TV, radio, and computers, their deeds were spread by word of mouth, or sometimes in books. Warriors, kings, and beautiful women were remembered in songs and in stories. But celebrity depends on widespread publicity, delivered quickly. It wasn't until the nineteenth century that industry provided the means for mass communication in the form of cheap printing and swift circulation.

Charles Dickens and His Fans

Author Charles Dickens was one of the first people to harness this new power. He decided to print his novels in cheaply produced magazines that ordinary people could afford. He published only a chapter at a time so that people had to wait for the next installment, creating a buzz about what was going to happen next. He also made public appearances, reading from his stories like an actor performing on a stage. He understood people's appetite for excitement and used the media to become one of the first celebrities.

Charles Dickens was one of the first writers to exploit the public's fascination with him as well as his novels.

Star Struck

During the first 20 years of the twentieth century, film stars began to emerge. Movie audiences began to identify their favorite actors, and the film studios quickly exploited this interest, managing the way these stars were presented to the public so that they were seen in the best possible light. However, fans wanted more. They wanted to know about the private lives of their screen idols.

Case Study: Clara Bow

Clara Bow emerged from a troubled, difficult childhood to become a famous Hollywood film actress in the 1920s after winning a beauty contest at the age of 16. She is often described as America's first sex symbol, largely because of her role in the 1927 film It. At the height of her fame, she received more than 45,000 fan letters a month. However, there were many rumors about her private life. The pressures of fame led to exhaustion and growing mental health problems. By the early 1930s, her career was over.

Clara Bow's sexy, spirited on-screen persona fueled many rumors about her off-screen personal life.

• Up for Discussion •

Clara Bow escaped from a harsh and difficult childhood to become a world-famous actress. However, the media were not always kind to her and often published unconfirmed rumors and lies. Why do you think they did this? Do you think this added to her appeal? Why?

Changing Attitudes

In the 1960s, there was a shift in public attitudes toward fame and celebrity. People were less in awe of those in power or those with money. As some of the rigid divisions in society broke down, ordinary people began to ask more questions. They challenged some of the traditional respect for those with wealth and influence.

The Record Industry

The ready availability of recorded music and the popularity of radio created many twentieth-century musical celebrities, the most famous of which included Elvis Presley and the Beatles.

Singing about love and life's hardships, these musicians connected with millions of ordinary listeners who wanted to know about their idols' experiences. The pop star was born.

Pop stars such as Elvis Presley attracted hysterical crowds wherever they played.

Case Study: The British Royals

People have always been fascinated by the British royal family. Yet until the 1960s, the private life of the Windsors remained strictly private, and few people had access to them. In 1969, the Queen allowed the BBC to film her family in a more informal way. The Royal Family, the first behind-the-scenes glimpse of royal life, intended to promote their activities in a positive light. Nearly 70 percent of the British public watched it. But after this, the media's attitude to the royals became increasingly disrespectful and intrusive. Newspapers began to speculate about their relationships and personal behavior. Members of the royal family had become celebrities—just like pop singers and film stars.

Prince Harry is often pursued by photographers on his nights out.

The Impact of Television

Television sets appeared in people's homes as early as the 1940s, but became increasingly common by the mid-1960s. Famous people now could be observed on a daily basis—what they wore, what they said, and how they behaved. Images were broadcast into millions of living rooms. Watching the stars became an everyday occurrence. But this new familiarity with celebrities did not lessen people's interest in them. Instead, it increased the public's appetite for fresh information about every aspect of their lives.

• Up for Discussion •

Royal families and presidential families are famous because of their very public roles and responsibilities. Should the media respect their privacy? What if family members behave inappropriately or deliberately draw attention to their private lives? Does this make them fair game in the media?

Playing the
Fame Game

Celebrities need the media. They need to be photographed and interviewed to stay in the public eye and maintain their high profile. A high profile can bring film roles, recording contracts, and lucrative advertising deals. Without a high profile, celebrity careers start to fade. So celebrities play the fame game to make sure they aren't forgotten.

The Media Tour

Celebrities use the media to promote themselves and what they do. They call press conferences, talk to journalists, wear designer clothes, and attend big events in order to be noticed. Actors and musicians are expected to promote their latest film or album by giving interviews and appearing on talk shows around the country or around the world. This is often written into their contracts for a project.

The Celebrity Stunt

Celebrities sometimes try to attract additional media attention by doing something that will ensure they are talked about. At the 2003 MTV music video awards show in New York, pop star Madonna kissed fellow singers Britney Spears and Christina Aguilera during their performance. This had been planned in advance with the show's producers. The stunt guaranteed huge media coverage for all three stars. It also completely overshadowed the performances of many other celebrities that night.

Britney Spears, Madonna, and Christina Aguilera perform on stage together at the 2003 MTV music video awards.

Case Study: I'm a Celebrity . . .

The game show I'm a Celebrity, Get Me Out of Here! *puts a group of celebrities into stressful situations in the jungle and invites viewers to vote for their favorites. The format is* used in several countries around the world. The participants tend to be minor celebrities trying to revive flagging careers with a new burst of publicity. It certainly worked for British model Katie Price and Australian singer Peter Andre, who met on the set and relaunched themselves as a celebrity couple with their own reality TV show. Katie Price's name has since become a brand that she uses to sell novels, DVDs, clothes, and other merchandise.

Katie Price and Peter Andre at the start of their relationship in 2004. When the couple's marriage ran into difficulties in 2009, both used the media to show how they were coping.

• Up for Discussion •

Madonna's stunt at the 2003 MTV music video awards attracted lots of attention. What did she hope to gain from this? What about the show's producers?

A Match Made in the Media

While celebrities depend on the media to keep them in the public eye, the media relies on celebrities to maintain or boost their audiences. The benefits are clear for both sides. Celebrities get publicity, and the media makes money. However, celebrities can make plenty of money from the media, too.

Doing a Deal

Exclusive deals with celebrities can keep magazines and TV shows ahead of their rivals in a fiercely competitive market. For example, *OK!* magazine's exclusive coverage of the wedding of Victoria and David Beckham in 1999 helped to sell a then record 1.5 million copies of the magazine. Readers bought it because they knew they wouldn't see the pictures anywhere else.

Celebrity exclusives don't come cheap, however. The bigger the star, the greater the cost. Magazines can expect to pay several million dollars for exclusive rights to publish celebrity wedding photos or the first pictures of a celebrity baby.

Everyone's a Winner?

Some people argue that such lucrative deals reward the people who least need the money. The wedding of wealthy actors Michael Douglas and Catherine Zeta-Jones was paid for entirely by *OK!* magazine's $2 million fee. However, it could be argued that such deals help to protect celebrities from an invasion of

Victoria Adams (Posh Spice) with David Beckham shortly after their engagement in 1998.

16

Case Study: The Bidding War

When celebrity couple Brad Pitt and Angelina Jolie announced that they were expecting twins, a bidding war broke out between rival magazines to gain the right to publish the first pictures of the babies. Hello! and the weekly magazine People eventually outbid OK! and jointly published the first pictures for a record-breaking $14 million, boosting sales of People to its highest level in recent years. The couple donated the money to a children's charity and generated huge publicity for themselves and their chosen cause. However, some critics suspected that Jolie had insisted on a purely positive portrayal of her family as part of the deal, potentially limiting the magazines' editorial independence.

Brad Pitt and Angelina Jolie, photographed traveling with their children in 2009.

privacy by unwelcome paparazzi. Also, some celebrities are known to donate their fees to charity. The publicity is good for them, as well as for the charity they are supporting.

• Up for Discussion •

Why is the public so eager to read about celebrity weddings and births?

Do you think the fees and the media coverage can detract from the significance of such events? In what ways?

Fifteen Minutes of Fame

Some celebrities have worked for years to make a name for themselves. Others seem to become famous overnight. Reality TV, in particular, has helped to create the instant celebrity—a person who is unknown one day and recognized by millions of people the next. A few of these people will have an agent or a publicist and start to build a career out of being famous. But many instant celebrities disappear just as quickly as they arrive.

Talent Shows

Television airs talent shows, such as *American Idol*, in which singers audition and compete for the chance to win a top recording contract and live the celebrity lifestyle. However, the producers often focus on the worst auditions or the most dramatic life stories because this is what audiences enjoy. Sometimes these failed contestants become celebrities themselves, not because they are talented, but simply because we recognize them from TV.

Problem TV

Some TV programs, such as *Dr. Phil,* encourage ordinary people to discuss their personal problems on air. Reality shows such as *Wife Swap* or *Nanny 911* take us directly into family homes and relationships. Producers say such programs help us to deal with our own problems by learning from others' mistakes. But the main purpose of these programs is to entertain us.

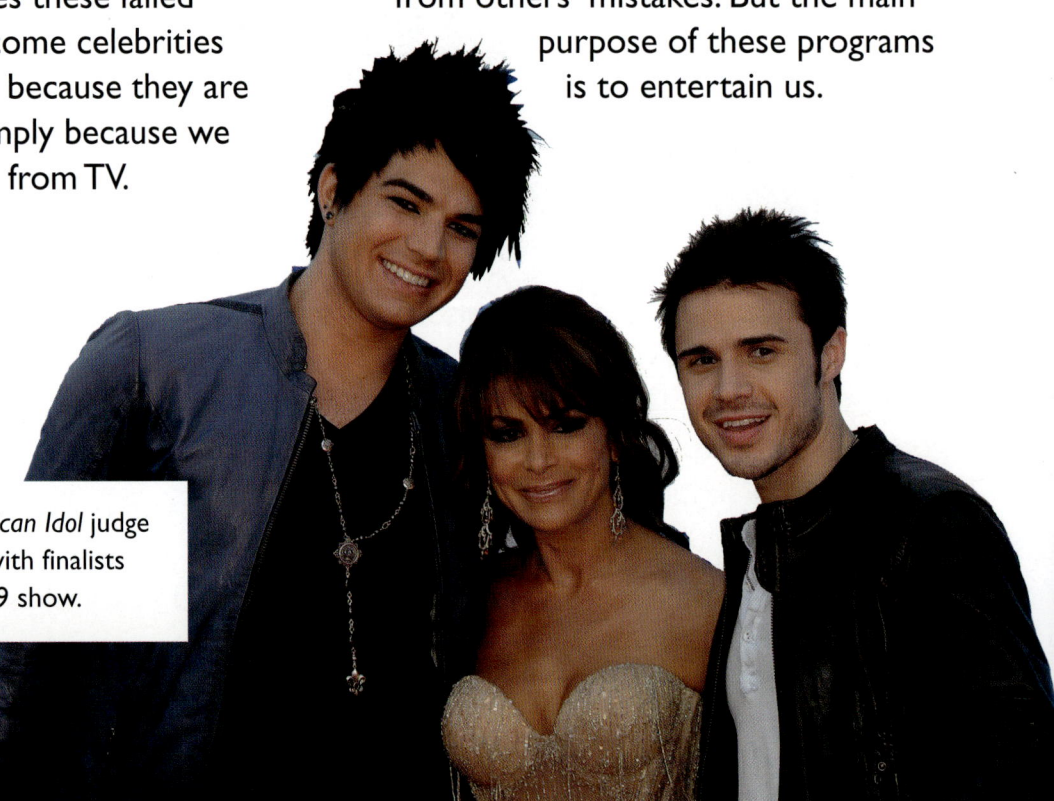

Former *American Idol* judge Paula Abdul with finalists from the 2009 show.

Case Study: Big Brother

The reality TV show Big Brother is produced in countries all around the world. Contestants are filmed living in a house together and audiences vote to evict their least favorite members. However, the producers have been criticized for choosing fame-hungry wannabes who are prepared to do anything to secure lucrative deals with the media when they leave the show. Producers are under pressure to choose entertaining characters, but this has often resulted in clashes of personality, violent arguments, and even accusations of racist behavior and sexual harassment from the contestants.

Transsexual Portuguese bank clerk Nadia Almada won the UK's Big Brother show in 2004. She went on to release a pop record and appear on numerous TV talk shows. She is currently writing a memoir.

• Up for Discussion •

Reality TV shows often show people in emotionally charged situations. These people have given their consent to filming. Does this make it acceptable to show everything?

Press Intrusion

People expect celebrities to be well groomed and glamorous, and celebrities aim to give them what they want at public events in front of the cameras. However, the private lives of celebrities often seem more fascinating than their public personas. How do the stars behave behind closed doors? Journalists and photographers know that we'll pay to find out.

On the Doorstep

Most countries have trespass laws that make it illegal for journalists and paparazzi to gain unauthorized access to private property. So they wait just outside a celebrity's home and film the person entering or leaving. They also push cameras up to the car windows and interview the neighbors in the hope of uncovering some new gossip or taking an image that shows the celebrity in a less-than-perfect light. Many celebrities claim that this aggressive pursuit verges on stalking, and some have taken legal action against photographers.

Secret Filming

Another tactic used by some paparazzi involves filming or taking photographs in secret. Photographers might use a telephoto lens to take pictures from a distance. Some have pretended to be ordinary members of the public. Celebrities are often photographed on beaches by paparazzi posing as tourists or lifeguards while using hidden cameras.

Paparazzi can resort to aggressive tactics to take pictures of celebrities who are out and about.

Case Study: Princess Diana

The tragic death of Princess Diana led to widespread calls for better regulation of the paparazzi.

In August 1997, Diana, Princess of Wales, was killed in a car accident in Paris after a high-speed chase involving several press photographers. Princess Diana had always attracted huge media attention as a beautiful and charismatic member of the British royal family. When she left her hotel that day with her boyfriend, Dodi Al-Fayed, the paparazzi pursued her. A later inquest into her death found that she had been unlawfully killed by the actions of her driver, who was drunk, and the press photographers who had tried to get close to her car as it sped through the streets. One of the most shocking facts to emerge from the tragedy was that the paparazzi, who had partly caused the accident, took photographs at the scene before the emergency services arrived.

• Up for Discussion •

The paparazzi say that their unofficial images act as extra publicity for celebrities. They point out that celebrities have chosen to expose themselves to public scrutiny and that it is not illegal to take pictures in a public place. But some celebrities think this amounts to stalking, which is illegal. What do you think?

A Step Too Far?

Celebrities respond to the pressures of fame in different ways. A few become reclusive, hiding from the cameras. Others seek escape through drugs and alcohol abuse. Many celebrities experience relationship difficulties and some can find their health affected by the strain of keeping up appearances.

Feeling the Pressure

Living in the glare of the media undoubtedly carries a mental and physical cost. This includes press intrusion, public speculation, and the pressure to look good, even when you are exhausted or depressed. Some celebrities blame the media when the strain begins to show. But these are the same stars who invited the photographers to their weddings and flaunted their successes at premieres and awards ceremonies. Can they expect to be left alone when it becomes too much?

Rest in Peace?

The greater the pain, the more the media pursue the story. The death of Michael Jackson in 2009 unleashed a media frenzy. Camera crews tracked the progress of the ambulance as it carried the pop star to UCLA Medical Center, and the media established itself outside the hospital once his death was confirmed.

Michael Jackson died of heart failure, allegedly as a result of the drugs he was taking to help him cope with the strain of a comeback concert tour in 2009.

When young actor River Phoenix died of a drug overdose in Los Angeles

Case Study: Britney Spears

Britney Spears spent her teenage years in the media spotlight, singing and performing on TV. By the time she was 18, she had a U.S. Number 1 hit. Over the next few years, she became a pop superstar. However, her personal life became increasingly chaotic as the paparazzi recorded her partying and unpredictable behavior.

In 2007, she shaved off her hair in front of the paparazzi in what many people saw as a desperate gesture. Later that year, her ex-husband, Kevin Federline, obtained sole custody of their two young children. In January 2008, Spears became hysterical and was taken to a psychiatric hospital. The entire scene was broadcast on TV. Her career did recover after this shocking event, but her father was granted temporary legal control over her.

BRITNEY SPEARS

BBC NEWS 24 08:31 REPUBLICAN FIELD

Britney Spears' removal from her home to a psychiatric hospital was filmed by waiting TV crews and broadcast around the world.

in 1993, someone broke into the building where his body lay in a casket and took a photograph. The image of the dead actor was later published in a gossip magazine, the *National Enquirer*.

• Up for Discussion •

Britney Spears appeared to invite publicity when she shaved her head in front of the cameras. Was the media right to respond by photographing her? What if celebrities are suffering from an addiction, mental illness, or a personal tragedy? Is there anything that the media shouldn't show?

Privacy Laws

Many celebrities would like to see the introduction of new laws to protect their privacy. When they are photographed with their babies during a quiet walk in a park, most people would agree with them. However, many journalists and media organizations argue that stricter laws would damage the freedom of the press.

Press Freedom

What if a famous politician is having an affair with a lawyer or a judge? What if a model says she is naturally thin but is actually anorexic? Should the media keep these a secret? Some people think that the public needs to know about celebrity behavior as it affects our trust in them. When California introduced new laws to protect its movie stars from being filmed or photographed where they had "a reasonable expectation of privacy," civil rights campaigners argued that this was a move against freedoms guaranteed in the U.S. Constitution.

Trade Secrets?

When celebrity actors Catherine Zeta-Jones and Michael Douglas were married in a private ceremony in New York in 2000, *OK!* magazine paid them for exclusive pictures of

Michael Douglas and Catherine Zeta-Jones are often happy to kiss for the cameras. However, they sued *Hello!* magazine for publishing unauthorized pictures of their wedding.

Case Study: Mitterand's Daughter

France has some of the strictest privacy laws in the world. The French media did not report the existence of former President Francois Mitterand's illegitimate daughter, despite the fact that they knew about it and that President Mitterand was married at the time and often posed for pictures with his legitimate children. However, in 1994, France's best-selling magazine Paris Match broke the silence and published pictures of his 20-year-old daughter, Mazarine. The magazine argued that Mitterand had brought such exposure on himself by allowing Mazarine to be seen with him in public. Yet many French politicians condemned Paris Match for its action.

French President Mitterand's illegitimate daughter, Mazarine Pingeot, went unreported for many years.

the event. However, a photographer from rival magazine *Hello!* snuck in and took pictures with a hidden camera. The couple sued *Hello!* over the secret pictures. The judge in the case agreed that such images were a "trade secret" and that the couple had a right to "commercial confidentiality." But they did not win substantial damages for invasion of privacy because they had allowed *OK!* to publish pictures of their wedding.

• Up for Discussion •

Is freedom of information more important than a celebrity's privacy? In what circumstances, if any, do you think celebrities should lose their right to privacy?

Lies, All Lies!

Our appetite for celebrity news seems never-ending. We don't want the same old stories. We want new information, new gossip, and new revelations. The media knows that if we don't get what we want, we'll stop reading, stop watching, and stop buying. Sometimes journalists and bloggers are tempted to make up a story about a celebrity. Who cares if it isn't true? It'll make a great headline.

Bad Press

Some believe "any publicity is good publicity," but it's not necessarily true. Most celebrities accept a certain amount of unfounded rumor and inaccurate reporting as the price they have to pay for their public status. But lies about the private lives of celebrities can destroy their popularity. Rumors about ill health can damage their career prospects. In 1999, actor Arnold Schwarzenegger won damages against a U.S. newspaper that printed that his heart was a "ticking time bomb" and that he was unfit to work. The story was simply not true.

Arnold Schwarzenegger (left) in the 1999 movie *End of Days*.

Case Study: "Freddie Starr Ate My Hamster!"

In 1986, the Sun, a UK newspaper, printed a shocking story that revealed how comedian Freddie Starr had eaten a hamster sandwich. But the story was untrue. Max Clifford, head of a successful PR company, later admitted that he had made it up in order to gain publicity for his client. His tactics certainly worked. "Freddie Starr ate my hamster!" became one of the most notorious headlines in British news and ensured that the comedian's name was not forgotten.

Freddie Starr was still posing for publicity photos like this one 10 years after the original hamster headline appeared in the *Sun* newspaper.

Libel Laws

Many countries have laws that permit people to sue the media—if they can prove that a story about them is untrue and has hurt their feelings or damaged their professional reputation. However, enforcing such laws isn't easy, particularly on the Internet. The celebrity gossip web site, Mr. Paparazzi, publishes stories sent in by members of the public, but it has a disclaimer that it is not responsible for the accuracy of such stories.

Similarly, members of the public sometimes come forward with "kiss and tell" stories to sell to newspapers and magazines. These stories may or not be true, but they are often published anyway. Editors rely on the fact that many celebrities won't sue for libel because they don't want their private lives to be scrutinized by the court.

• Up for Discussion •

Is it wrong for the media to publish rumor and gossip as fact? What about celebrities who release false information to gain publicity?

The Mr. Paparazzi web site says that it is not responsible for the accuracy of stories sent in by members of the public. Should it be? What's your view?

A Public Fascination

What is it about celebrities that we find so fascinating? We don't know them, or socialize with them, or have them as friends. Yet they wouldn't exist if we weren't interested. Perhaps we are attracted to them because they are not like us. They offer a fantasy, an escape from our everyday lives.

Case Study: Cribs

The show Cribs, formerly known as MTV Cribs, takes viewers on a tour of celebrity homes. The stars reveal their swimming pools, their bedrooms, and even the contents of their refrigerator. Popular since it first aired in 2000, *Cribs offers a tantalizing glimpse of celebrity lifestyles as well as great publicity for featured stars who get to show their "real" selves— carefully made-up and fully stage-managed, of course!*

The luxurious home of singer Mariah Carey in Bel Air, Los Angeles.

Love to Hate Them

Beautiful, successful, rich, famous—celebrities seem to have it all. They wear the clothes that people want to wear, drive the cars that people want to own, and live lifestyles that most people can only dream about. But while some people want their favorite stars to remain perfect forever, many people also enjoy finding out about celebrities on their bad days, recovering from plastic surgery, or cheating on their spouses. Perhaps audiences seek out these stories because it makes them feel better about their own lives. Certainly, tabloid magazines such as *Globe* and *Star* exploit this interest by publishing incriminating images under headlines such as "He Cheated in Rehab" and "He Asks Mistress to Marry Him."

Keeping Up with Celebrity News

Star gossip, conjecture, and confirmed celebrity news has a niche of its own. In addition to the magazines and tabloids, the E! television channel and its web site are dedicated to celebrity news and sightings. *Entertainment Tonight* and *Hard Copy* also present information and videos of celebrities. Most newspapers have some entertainment news. These may include interviews, reviews, and photos. It seems that we just can't get enough of the celebrities.

Actress Jessica Biel hides her face from the cameras while walking her dog.

• Up for Discussion •

Does it matter if stories about celebrities are taking up newspaper space and airtime that could be given to more serious investigative news?

Should news entertain us or educate us? Can there be a balance? What do you think?

Celebrity and Me

The media doesn't just feed our appetite for celebrity news. It also encourages us to try to become famous ourselves. Talent shows, modeling competitions, and other forms of reality TV invite us to "be discovered."

I Want it Too!

Some people seek fame even though they aren't talented singers, actors, or athletes. They try to attach themselves to celebrities by hanging out at the same parties, going out with them, or becoming part of their entourage as a way to access their celebrity lifestyles. The media encourage this sense of entitlement by bombarding us with images of successful, glamorous people.

A Virtual Relationship

Some fans idolize their favorite celebrities. They build up huge expectations and invest a great deal of time, money, and emotion in pursuing their obsession. But what happens when things go wrong? Celebrities may die, or split up, or otherwise disappoint their public. When boy band Take That announced their split in 1996, special phone helplines were set up to counsel distressed fans. When singer Elvis Presley died in 1977, some grief-stricken fans refused to believe that he had actually died.

Take That performs their final single, "How Deep Is Your Love?" at the 1996 Brit Awards. The band reformed in 2006.

Case Study: American Idol and the X Factor

The makers of American Idol and its UK counterpart, the X Factor, are frequently criticized for the ritualized humiliation of weaker contestants and the manipulation of ordinary people's desire for fame. Certainly, the judges' comments often seem intended to shock or entertain rather than offer constructive feedback. Sometimes, this has serious consequences. Paula Goodspeed, an obsessive Paula Abdul fan, was heavily criticized by the judges during her audition for American Idol. Abdul, a judge on the show, claimed that she warned producers of the contestant's troubling behavior before the audition took place, but filming went ahead anyway. Some months later, Goodspeed committed suicide outside Abdul's home.

A young contestant auditions during the 2008 season of *American Idol* in Hollywood, California.

• Up for Discussion •

The producers of *American Idol* cannot be expected to assess the mental state of each contestant. But should judges be allowed to criticize members of the public in such a personal way on national TV in the name of entertainment? What's your view?

Identity Crisis

We often expect our celebrities to be thin, beautiful, and wrinkle-free. Certainly, this is the way they are presented to us in advertising, in films, and on TV. But such beauty is rarely achieved without extreme dieting or exercise, a team of makeup artists, expensive treatments, and surgery or careful digital editing of photos to remove those unwanted bulges and blemishes.

Get the Look

Celebrity looks, clothes, and lifestyles create aspirations. This is why advertisers like to use celebrities to promote their products. We want what they have. There's nothing wrong with copying a "look"—a haircut, a dress shape—but at what price? For some people, the desire to dress like their favorite stars and live the celebrity lifestyle becomes an intolerable pressure to buy things they can't afford. This can lead to serious problems with debt and risks, causing a crippling sense of dissatisfaction and depression.

Celebrity heiress and professional party girl Paris Hilton promotes her latest perfume Can Can at Selfridges in London in May 2008.

Case Study: "I Want a Famous Face"

Some people become so obsessed with particular celebrities that they are prepared to undergo plastic surgery to look more like them. Noses, breasts, jaws, abdomens—all they need is a surgeon to carry out the work and enough money to pay for it. Reality TV shows, such as MTV's I Want A Famous Face, follow young adults as they undergo the harrowing procedures. The dangers of surgery are routinely pointed out during these programs, but critics argue that they encourage viewers to question their own looks.

Earnest Valentino, a Michael Jackson impersonator, has undergone extensive facial surgery to look like his late idol.

A Dangerous Obsession

For some people, the pressure to look a certain way creates a loss of self-esteem. Everyone is unique, but sometimes the desire for success, approval, and admiration means that we are prepared to put ourselves through plastic surgery or a diet so extreme that it leads to an eating disorder such as anorexia. The top models and film actors are predominantly thin and fair-skinned. This has created a market for skin-whitening creams and diet pills that can harm consumers' health and well-being.

• Up for Discussion •

Media outlets could choose to present a more realistic and balanced view of beauty to their audiences, but most of the time they do not. Why is this?

Taking Sides

The media frequently manipulate stories about celebrities to make them more exciting or more shocking. But celebrities manipulate the media, too. They may willingly conduct their private struggles and family arguments in the public eye to punish their opponents and win sympathy for themselves and generate publicity in the process. After all, their reputations are at stake. If one side is to look good, the other side will have to look bad. Who will win in the court of public opinion?

A Very Public Argument

When ordinary families disagree, they don't usually air their problems in public. However, a celebrity spat creates huge media interest. Some celebrities try to control the rumors and the gossip by going on the attack. When actress Lindsay Lohan's father publicly expressed his disapproval about her love life, she hit back by calling him "a public embarrassment" on her MySpace page. Her comments were published on celebrity gossip sites within seconds.

PR Spin

Celebrities often hire publicists to manage bad news such as an impending divorce. Interviews are booked to allow the celebrities to give their side of the story. Sympathetic photo shoots are arranged to show celebrities looking brave or poignant or doting on their children. Celebrities may even leak voice mail and text messages from their former partners to persuade the public that they've been treated badly and deserve our support.

Lindsay Lohan and her father, Michael Lohan, have used the media to argue with each other in public.

Case Study: Paul McCartney and Heather Mills

Attempts to manipulate public opinion through the media do not always succeed. Former Beatles member Paul McCartney and his wife Heather Mills announced their decision to divorce in 2006, citing media intrusion as a reason for the split. However, when details of Heather Mills' personal accusations against Paul McCartney were leaked to the press, the media interest intensified. Heather Mills not only used the media to convey her feelings about McCartney, but also hit back during an interview on TV against the tabloid newspapers who had published a series of unfavorable stories about her. When the divorce settlement was announced, she tried to stop publication of the judgment by arguing that it was an invasion of privacy. She was overruled.

Heather Mills talks to the media outside the High Court after she reached a divorce settlement with Paul McCartney.

• Up for Discussion •

Paul McCartney refused to comment after the announcement of his divorce settlement with Heather Mills. His good reputation was largely maintained. Was this due to his silence in the face of Mills' outbursts? Or was it due to the fact that Heather Mills was never going to win a popularity vote against a much-loved former Beatle?

Child Stars

Sometimes children become celebrities. They may have risen to fame because of their talents as actors, singers, or athletes. They may have starred in a reality TV program, or they may have acquired their celebrity status simply because their parents are famous. Their lives may seem exciting, but many people question the benefits of celebrity for children who don't yet have the maturity to deal with its downside.

Out of the Limelight

Many celebrity parents try to protect their children from the glare of the media. They do everything they can to preserve their anonymity, hiding them from the cameras, and insisting on privacy clauses in contracts with nannies and housekeepers. Angelina Jolie gave birth to her twins in France where laws protecting the privacy of celebrities are particularly strict. Most of the time, the media respect such wishes. However, those who are under 18 and deliberately place themselves in the spotlight are not always treated so carefully.

Too Much Too Young?

Miley Cyrus and Peaches Geldof emerged from the shadows of famous parents and chose careers in front of the cameras before their eighteenth birthdays. However, Miley Cyrus' wholesome Disney image was tarnished when she allowed herself to be photographed bare-backed and apparently topless for *Vanity Fair* magazine. Peaches Geldof was rarely out of the gossip columns after presenting her own TV

UK diver Tom Daley faced intense media interest when he competed in the Beijing Olympics at 14. He was bullied at school when he returned home.

Case Study: The Osbournes

Teenagers Kelly and Jack Osbourne shot to fame when they appeared in a reality TV show about life with their famous parents, Ozzy and Sharon Osbourne. The cameras were allowed into the Osbourne family home. Jack and Kelly were shown swearing, joking, and fighting throughout several highly successful series. Despite their struggles with addiction and Jack's depression, both have forged solo celebrity careers. However, their elder sister Aimee has always refused to participate in the family's on-screen activities and as a result does not have the same celebrity profile.

Kelly and Jack Osbourne play up to the cameras at the MTV Movie Awards in Los Angeles, California, in 2002.

show at 16. Some people argue that children and teenagers should not be exposed to the glare of the media because they cannot be expected to anticipate how their comments and behavior will be reported, scrutinized, and manipulated.

• Up for Discussion •

Ozzy and Sharon Osbourne invited TV cameras into their home when their son Jack was only 13. Were they right to do so? What do you think?

Would you like to take part in a reality TV show? Why? What effect do you think it might have on you?

Doing Good

Celebrities have to look after their own interests, but this doesn't mean that they can't help others, too. Some famous people use their popularity and high profile in the media to promote the work of charities, support government campaigns, and publicize good causes.

Role Models

Celebrities are often chosen to front a campaign or represent a charity because they are seen as good role models who will raise the profile of the cause they support. This may be because they strive to achieve their goals, work tirelessly to help others, or behave considerately in their sport or profession. Oprah Winfrey topped a U.S. list of celebrity role models in 2006 after she donated $40 million to the Oprah Winfrey Leadership Academy for Girls in South Africa.

Oprah Winfrey opened a new Leadership Academy for Girls in South Africa in 2007.

Fundraising

Famous people often appear at charity events, usually performing for free to maximize profits for the charity concerned. Their celebrity status attracts attention and ticket sales from people who might not otherwise support charities, such as those that help people living in poverty or with HIV/AIDS. A British charity, Comic Relief, collaborates with the BBC to broadcast a series of stunts and comic performances interspersed with appeals by celebrities asking viewers to donate money. Some people think celebrities use it to further their own careers. Nevertheless, in 2009, Comic Relief raised approximately $107 million to help poor and disadvantaged people around the world.

British deejay Aled Jones poses with members of the girl band the Saturdays, at the official launch of Comic Relief's Red Nose Day in 2009.

• Up for Discussion •

Some fundraisers are criticized by people who feel the extravagance of such events sends the wrong message about charity. Others point out that such events raise lots of money for charity as well as publicizing their cause. What do you think?

Case Study: Live 8

Live 8, a series of concerts, held on July 2, 2005, aimed to put pressure on world leaders to reduce the debts of the world's poorest nations. The concerts were free as their purpose was not to raise money for charity, but to publicize the crisis of poverty and persuade politicians to bring about change. Hundreds of celebrity acts performed at outdoor venues around the world including London, Philadelphia, and Sydney. The concerts achieved maximum publicity and helped to raise public awareness, but some critics felt that celebrities' profiles benefited most from the concerts. Live 8 did little to change government policy or improve the lives of ordinary people in developing countries.

The Future of Celebrity

The current obsession with celebrity is encouraged by the media who are hungry for a share of the audience—that's us. Will our fascination with the rich and famous continue to grow? We don't appear to have tired of them yet. Continuing advances in digital media simply feed the public appetite for more gossip, more glamour, and more scandal.

A Dumbed-down Media?

There's only so much news we can absorb. So why not combine the celebrity format with more serious news? Journalists who research hard news know that finding a celebrity angle will help to get their stories aired. Politicians, meanwhile, are increasingly using the entertainment media to put across their message. Barack Obama was the first U.S. president to appear on a TV talk show while in office. He's unlikely to be the last.

Fans take photos of the Manchester United soccer team with their cell phones and digital cameras.

We're All Paparazzi Now

Phones with cameras and Internet access are everywhere these days. Members of the public can snap an image of a celebrity and forward it to a picture agency in just seconds. Splash picture agency encourages people to "snap, send, and tell." Celebrity web sites such as Mr. Paparazzi and Digital Spy depend on an interactive audience for their news stories. Ordinary individuals increasingly participate in the cult of celebrity to make money and a name for themselves.

Case Study: Jade Goody

Jade Goody rose to fame as an ill-informed and outspoken contestant on the UK's Big Brother show. Her growing media profile meant that she returned to a celebrity version of the show in 2007, but she was publicly reviled for some allegedly racist comments about a fellow contestant. During another live show in India in 2008, she was told that she had cervical cancer. Public sympathy for her began to grow. She allowed the TV cameras to record her last months in order to make as much money as possible for her two young sons. She made no secret of the fact that her illness was terminal, but many people felt OK! magazine went too far when it published its memorial issue before she died.

Jade Goody waves to the cameras just a month before she died in March 2009.

• Up for Discussion •

Jade Goody lived her life in the media spotlight. Some feel that she did much to raise awareness of cervical cancer in the UK. Yet she also used the media to make lots of money. So was she a brave campaigner, a fame-hungry wannabe, or a vulnerable and ill young woman who should have been allowed to die in private? What's your view?

Glossary

anonymity Being unknown to the general public.

aspiration A strong wish or desire for something.

bidding war Rival buyers bid against each other for the right to publish an exclusive story or photographs.

blog A web log or online journal.

broadcast To publish in the media.

celebrities Those who become famous through high exposure in the media or who use the media to maintain their public profiles.

commercial confidentiality The right to keep something secret in order to protect your investment.

consent Permission.

copyright A law that makes it illegal to use someone else's images or words without their permission.

counsel To give advice or guidance to someone.

damages Financial compensation decided by a court.

disclaimer A statement denying responsibility for something.

eating disorder A psychological problem to do with eating, such as anorexia or bulimia.

editorial independence The media's freedom to publish what they like without interference from anyone else.

endorsed Publicly approved of or backed by someone.

exclusive A story or an image that no other media outlet has access to.

exploit To make the best use of a person or situation.

format The arrangement and content of a publication or TV program.

hard news News about serious subjects such as crime, conflict, and government.

idol A person who is widely adored and revered.

illegitimate Born outside of marriage.

intrusion Invading someone's privacy.

leak Reveal to the media unofficially or anonymously.

libel The crime of publishing lies about someone through the media.

lucrative Profitable.

manipulate Interfere with to make something appear in a certain way.

memoir The story of a person's life as told by them.

merchandise Products for sale.

paparazzi Photographers who take pictures of celebrities, often without their permission.

persona Character, image.

PR Public relations; the business of dealing with the media.

promote To attract publicity for an event or product.

publicist Someone who manages the publicity for a celebrity or an event.

publicity Putting information out to the general public to promote a person, event, or product.

racist The belief that one race of people is superior to another race of people.

reality TV Programs that use real life situations and people who are not actors to provide entertainment.

role model A famous person admired by the public.

sex symbol A celebrity who is widely acknowledged to have lots of sex appeal.

sexual harassment Unwelcome attention that is sexual in nature.

speculate To guess.

stalking Obsessive or relentless pursuit of someone.

sue To go to court in order to claim damages.

Further Information

Books

Burn, Kelli S. *Celebrity 2.0: How Social Media Foster Our Fascination With Popular Culture.* ABC-CLIO, LLC, 2009.

Hibbert, Adam. *The Power of the Media.* What's Your View? Smart Apple Media, 2007.

Wilson, Rosie. *Media and Communications Industry.* A Closer Look: Global Industries. Rosen Central, 2011.

Web Sites

http://entertainment.howstuffworks.com/tabloid2.htm
Information about the origin of tabloids, tabloids today, and libel.

http://www.eonline.com/
E! Online is an entertainment web site on the latest celebrity news.

http://www.sciencemuseum.org.uk
In the Search box, enter: spying on celebrities and select that PDF for a fun and informative game on the subject of privacy for celebrities. Choose one of six role play cards (such as a newspaper editor, a film star, a photographer, or a lawyer) and argue your case. The final page provides discussion questions.

http://www.howstuffworks.com/paparazzi.htm
This site discusses how the paparazzi work.

Note to parents and teachers: Every effort has been made by the publishers to ensure that these web sites are suitable for children, are of the highest educational value, and contain no inappropriate or offensive material. However, because of the nature of the Internet, it is impossible to guarantee that the contents of these sites will not be altered. We strongly advise that Internet access be supervised by a responsible adult.

Index

Numbers in bold refer to captions to illustrations.

A–B
Abdul, Paula 18, 31
actors 8, 10, 11, 14, 30, 33, 36
advertising 8, 14, 32
Aguilera, Christina 14, **14**
alcohol abuse 22
Andre, Peter 15, **15**
athletes (see also sports stars) 30, 36
BBC 13, 39
Beatles, the 12, 35
Beckham, David 9, 16, **16**
Beckham, Victoria 16, **16**
Biel, Jessica **29**
blogs 8, 9, **9**, 26
books 10, **10**, 15
Bow, Clara 11, **11**

C–E
Carey, Mariah **28**
celebrities
  attitudes toward 12–13
  legal action 20, 24, 25, 26, 27
  lifestyle 18, 28, 29, 30, 32
  looks 22, 32–33
  private lives 9, 10, 11, **11**, 13, 20, 26, 27, 34
  publicity 8, 10, 14, 15, 16, 17, 21, 23, 26, 27, **27**, 28, 34, 39
  relationships 13, 15, **15**, 16, 17, 18, 22, 24, 34, 35
  role models 38–39
charity 17, 38, 39
child stars 36–37
Clifford, Max 27
clothes 14, 15, 29, 32
contracts 14, 18, 36
copyright 9
Cyrus, Miley 36
Daley, Tom 36, **36**
Diana, Princess of Wales 21, **21**
Dickens, Charles 10, **10**
Douglas, Michael 16, 24, **24**
drugs 22, **22**
editors 27, 29
exclusives 9, 16, 24

F–I
fans 10, 11, 30, 31, **40**
film 8, 10, 11, 13, 14, 24, 26, 32, 33
Geldof, Peaches 36
Goody, Jade 41, **41**
gossip 8, 9, 20, 23, 26, 27, 34, 36, 40
Harry, Prince of Wales 13
headlines 26, 27, **27**
Hilton, Paris **32**
Hilton, Perez 9, **9**
Hollywood 9, 11, **31**
Internet 27, 40
interviews 14, 20, 34, 35

J–L
Jackson, Michael 22, **22**, 33
Jolie, Angelina 17, **17**, 36
journalists 14, 20, 24, 26, 29, 40
laws 20, 24, 25, 27, 36
libel 27
Live 8 39
Lohan, Lindsay 34, **34**

M–N
Madonna 14, **14**, 15
magazines 8, 9, 10, 16, 17, 23, 24, **24**, 25, 27, 29, 36, 41
  Heat 29
  Hello! 17, **24**, 25
  OK! 16, 17, 24, 25, 41
  Paris Match 25
  People 17
  Vanity Fair 36
McCartney, Paul 35, **35**
media
  coverage 14, 16, 17
  intrusion 22, 35
  lies 11, 26–27
merchandise 15
Miller, Sienna **8**
Mills, Heather 35, **35**
Mitterand, Francois 25
money 12, 16, 17, 24, 30, 33, 39, 40, 41
musicians (see also pop stars, rock stars, singers) 14, 30
MySpace 34
news bulletins 29
newspapers 8, 9, 10, 13, 26, 27, **27**, 29, 35
  Sun 27, **27**

O–P
Obama, Barack 40
Osbourne family 37
paparazzi 9, 17, 20, **20**, 21, **21**, 23, 40
Phoenix, River 22
photographers 9, **13**, 20, 21, 22, 25
picture agencies 9, 40
Pitt, Brad 17, **17**
plastic surgery 29, 33, **33**
politicians 24, 25, 39, 40
pop stars 12, **12**, 14, 22, 23, 30
Presley, Elvis 12, **12**, 30
press conferences 14
press freedom 24
Price, Katie 15, **15**
privacy 9, 13, 17, 24–25, 35, 36
producers 14, 15, 18, 19, 31
publicists 18, 34

R–S
radio 10, 12
reality TV 15, 18, 19, 30, 31, 33, 36, 37, 41
  Big Brother 19, **19**, 41
rock stars 8
royal family 13, 21
Schwarzenegger, Arnold 26, **26**
singers 15, 18, 28, 30, 36
Spears, Britney 14, **14**, 23, **23**
sports stars 8, 38, **40**
stalking 20, 21
Starr, Freddie 27, **27**

T–Z
Take That 30, **30**
talent shows 18, 30
  American Idol 18, **18**, 31, **31**
  X Factor 31
talk shows 14, 19, 40
television 8, 9, 10, 13, 15, 16, 18, 19, **19**, 23, **23**, 28, 30, 31, 32, 33, 35, 36, 37, 40, 41
video 9, 14, **14**, 15
web sites 9, 27, 29, 34, 40
  Mr. Paparazzi 27, 40
Winfrey, Oprah 38, **38**
Zeta-Jones, Catherine 16, 24, **24**

Explore the other titles in the *Media Power* series.

Sports

Master Drivers	8
Using the Media	10
Global Games	12
Big Business	14
"Show Me the Money"	16
Sports Idols	18
Shooting Stars	20
Crossing Over	22
High Pressure	24
Making Headlines	26
Media Overkill	28
Sports Scandals	30
Pushing the Boundaries	32
The Race Game	34
Fighting Discrimination	36
Tackling Inequality	38
Future Stories	40
Glossary	42
Further Information	43
Index	44

Crime

Crime: A Public Interest	8
What's New?	10
Fighting Crime	12
Your Call Counts!	14
The Thrill of the Chase	16
Balanced Reporting	18
Hidden Bias	20
Glamorizing Crime	22
Fiction or Real Life?	24
The Media Stunt	26
Name and Shame	28
Trial by Media	30
A Cause of Crime?	32
Checkbook Journalism	34
Under Surveillance	36
Crime Online	38
Power and Influence	40
Glossary	42
Further Information	43
Index	44

Celebrity and Fame

Media and Celebrity	8
The First Celebrities	10
Changing Attitudes	12
Playing the Fame Game	14
A Match Made in the Media	16
Fifteen Minutes of Fame	18
Press Intrusion	20
A Step Too Far?	22
Privacy Laws	24
Lies, All Lies!	26
A Public Fascination	28
Celebrity and Me	30
Identity Crisis	32
Taking Sides	34
Child Stars	36
Doing Good	38
The Future of Celebrity	40
Glossary	42
Further Information	43
Index	44

Causes and Campaigns

Campaigning and the Media	8
Money Talks	10
Disaster!	12
Raising the Roof	14
The Right Face	16
A Voice for the Voiceless	18
Two Sides to the Story	20
Conflicting Causes	22
Slow Burn	24
Straight Talk	26
The Media as Campaigner	28
Making News	30
Scare Tactics	32
Giving the People What They Want?	34
A Bad Light	36
Taking on the Media	38
Make the Media Work for You	40
Glossary	42
Further Information	43
Index	44

Politics

Politics and the Media	8
Who Owns the Media?	10
Fair and Balanced?	12
A Different Perspective	14
A Free Press?	16
Censorship	18
Open Access	20
Spin	22
The Right Look?	24
Questioning the Politician	26
Talk Radio	28
Politics as Entertainment	30
News Around the Clock	32
Newspaper Favoritism	34
Getting it Wrong	36
National or Local?	38
The Future	40
Glossary	42
Further Information	43
Index	44

War and Conflict

Reporting War and Conflict	8
Eyewitness	10
In the Frame	12
An Impartial View	14
Embedded Reporting	16
Spinning the Story	18
Propaganda	20
Censorship	22
The Terrorist's Tool	24
Choose Your Words	26
Stirring Up Hatred	28
A Moral Duty	30
In the Line of Fire	32
Look Away Now	34
Public Trust	36
Dramatizing Conflict	38
Media Audiences	40
Glossary	42
Further Information	43
Index	44